MW00977202

Long Days of Summer

in Evans County, Georgia

Lone Sentinel. (Acrylics on canvas).

Long Days of Summer
in Evans County, Georgia

Chloe Mitchell

Long Days of Summer in
Evans County, Georgia

Chloe Mitchell

Copyright © 2018
All rights reserved.

ISBN-10: 1982007281
ISBN-13: 978-1982007287

First Printing, 2018

Printed in the United States of America

Cover and Layout Design: Pharris Johnson

All paintings featured in this book are
by Chloe Mitchell.

DEDICATION

To the people of "The Level"

Contents

Introduction

Long Days of Summer in Evans County, Georgia is a collection of Chloe Perry Mitchell's memories of African Americans who lived near Hagan, Georgia, in a rural farm community referred to as "The Level." Mrs. Mitchell's affection for her colorful neighbors can be sensed as you read of the relationships of these people to her family. She demonstrates a passion for each individual in every vivid detail described for her readers.

Chloe Mitchell has a distinct memory of the events that occurred among The Level people. These individuals did not appear to be aware of discrimination, segregation, Jim Crowism and other injustices that were being protested by activists in other parts of the country. Many were not even aware of Dr. Martin Luther King, Jr.'s famous "I Have a Dream" speech. Life for them, on the surface, was simple. During the day they worked from dawn to dusk. On evenings and weekends they enjoyed church, listening to music, exchanging tales and frolicking. They had a special relationship with the people they worked for and for each other. They had a caring nature that extended to the landlords and their families.

For example, Cooter Mincey was more concerned with helping Mr. Ed Perry recuperate from his heart attack than focusing on what was happening outside The Level community. They were either not aware of the racial tension that existed in places in America like Money, Alabama, where the wrongful death of Emmett Till took place or since they were not directly affected, it was not an overriding concern.

There were no protests against racial injustices that were a part of the Jim Crow culture, because The Level's residents' basic needs were met, and they had a fondness for people like the Perry family. The individuals included in Mrs. Mitchell's writing shared love and not hate which transcended color lines.

This book exemplifies Chloe Mitchell's writing talents, and her accomplished skill as a folk artist. She taught herself to paint and the resulting heartwarming paintings included in this publication focus on her childhood memories.

Various members of the Evans County Historical Society and Evans County Afro-American Society have encouraged publication of this work. Chloe Mitchell, Doris Tomblin and Pharris Johnson served on the committee responsible for bringing this book to print.

The Evans County Afro-American Society was founded in 1985 by Ron Tomblin, Waymon Moody and the late Charles Bailey. This organization was established for the purpose of preserving the heritage and culture of people of African descent.

Doris Tomblin

Characters in the Stories

Theron Anderson — who Cooter called "Cleon." He was brother to Willie, Troy, and Buddy Anderson. Descendants of this family still live in Evans County.

Allie Mae Bacon — was the wife of Lawrence Bacon. Lawrence had a number of brothers including Landis Bacon. Landis had over 100 grandchildren and great-great grandchildren.

Herman and Lillie Belle (Smith?) — lived next to the Perry Pond, and were a young couple who worked hard, but also enjoyed their music.

Harley Brown — lived many years on the west side of Hagan. Jack, Purley, Waldo, and Mae were part of his family. Waldo worked for Dr. Ben Daniel, Jr. when Dr. Ben moved back to Claxton from Florida.

Mittie Brown (nicknamed "Doll Baby") — worked for Mona Lee Perry. Mittie moved from The Level to Reidsville and lived there until her death. She was married to Dan Collins, and they had four children.

Jonas Brewton — a former slave, was freed by his owner Samuel Brewton and continued to work for him after the war.

Rosa Brewton — wife of Willie Brewton. She and Willie had a grandson, James Brewton, who lives in the area. Rosa is local resident Louise Wilkerson's great-great aunt.

Willie Brewton — was the son of Jonas Brewton. Willie married Rosa.

Minnie Daniel — wife of Dr. Ben E. Daniel, Sr., was mother to Mona Lee and Dr. Ben Daniel, Jr. She lived in Claxton next door to the two-story brick school on Main Street (Highway 280).

Ruthie Mae Davis — had several children, lived in a house at the pecan orchard of the Perry Farm until they moved away to sharecrop. She died about 2012.

George Fagin — was about 100 years-old in the early 1960's. He was a small man, lean, his face slightly sagged, and his fingers greatly bowed backwards from handling so many pocketknives. He bought and resold these knives.

Mary and Cleve Hagan — were the parents of 10 children, one being Thaddeus. They lived next door to Cora and Thaddeus on Cleve Hagan Road, that was then known Perry Road.

Jack Littles – a small man who worked hard to keep food on his family's table. According to Cora Hagan, he lived across the Canoochee River and his brother lived in Claxton.

R.S. Lovett – over six feet tall, strong and proud, and worked hard to get ahead in timber cutting. He lived on Jones Street in Claxton and was a devout member of The Level Church. One of his sons, Marvin, is carrying on the family timber business.

"Cooter" Virgil Mincey – lived on the Perry Farm and later died in a nursing home.

Ernest Mitchell – lived next door to the Perry Pond on Perry Road and had a Geechee wife.

Anna Oxendine – washed and ironed for Minnie Daniel for many years. She and her family lived in Claxton. She married Orin Oxendine and they had four boys, four girls, and over a hundred grand and great-grand children. She was affectionately called "Big Mama" and died at the age of 82.

Ed Perry – owner of the Perry Farm close to Hagan, married Mona Lee Daniel. They moved into the Baker Daniel house and raised four children, Chloe, Malcolm, Ben, and Patricia.

Bob Small – lived to 104 years of age, and was father of 15 children, one being Cora Small Hagan.

Cora Small – married Thaddeus Hagan. Thaddeus is now deceased, but Cora still lives in The Level on Cleve Hagan Road. They have eight children, nine grandchildren and several great-grandchildren.

Aubrey Strickland – a local retired banker and a descendant of Samuel Brewton. Aubrey carried vegetables and other foods to share with Jonas. Samuel was first buried on what became Aubrey's farm and was later moved to Brewton Cemetery.

Willie and Annie Strowbridge – Annie and Willie Strowbridge were a married couple who lived in Bellville. They helped Mona Lee Perry with her yard work and later their son, Frank, assisted as well.

History of The Level

Tradition holds that Rev. Wyatt Kennedy (before c. 1860) led the founding of Eureka Congregationalist Church and "The Level" about 1880, which was the beginning of that community. Deacon John Kennedy, son of the founder, helped to carry on there for many years.

"The Level" is roughly the area below Bull Creek, south of Hagan, down to Bay Branch Church Road and over past Herbert Daniel's farm. It is truly level except where it falls off to Bull Creek and its tributaries. The church and cemetery are just below Bull Creek, about 3 miles south of Hagan. That Church later became Methodist and was called Mount Zion, of which Martha Murphy is said to have been the "Mother" for many years.

The African-American Camp Ground, also in that section of the county (on or near the Baker Brewton place and Smith Brothers' Pond), is thought to have been started in the latter part of the 19th century. It is said to have been a large shingle-covered shelter surrounded by camphouses, in use until about 1940. Camp Ground Church, later located near there, is still in use.

Dan K. Kennedy, also of The Level community, and promoter of various enterprises including a telephone system, a cotton gin, sawmill and a railroad (from Dean to his proposed town of Galilee on Carter Branch), succeeded in getting the Galilee post office and with his daughter Mamie operated it during the few months it was there, having a carrier from Hagan. Kennedy bargained for the land on which to build his town and had a big gathering on auction day, but the lots failed to sell and his town venture was a failure. His school and cannery located across the road from the Good Samaritan Lodge at The Level operated for a short time. Its opening was announced in the Claxton Enterprise, Aug. 1-1914, as follows:

> The Liberty Normal and Industrial School conducted for Negroes by D. K. Kennedy and his wife, colored, 4 miles south of Hagan, began operation of their canning factory on June first and is putting up six hundred cans each week. The products are placed in tin and consist

of apples, sweet potatoes, tomatoes and blackberries.
Nice apple jelly and peach juice is put in glass. The
products are sold to wholesale houses and reach the
market under the school brand.

Kennedy traveled to New York and other cities where he
gathered new ideas. He learned to make cement building blocks
(such as are manufactured in the county today) which he planned
to use in buildings and street-paving at Galilee. He also made
ornamental urns some of which may be seen at homes in this
section today. He lacked advanced education but is said to have
purchased a library and studied on his own.

Source of this history: *A History of Evans County Georgia*, Dorothy
Durrence Simmons, 1999.

Long Days of Summer in
Evans County, Georgia

1

Jonas

It was a sweltering day in Georgia in 1865 when the slaves were freed, a day when some danced a jig in honor of their freedom and yet some felt a sadness that they would be moving away from those they'd known all their lives.

On the Samuel Brewton Farm, though some stayed, Samuel watched his former workers leave with their household possessions hung in large sacks on their backs, some with sheets tied like cotton sheets slung over their shoulders. Muscled arms also pushed homemade wheelbarrows down the rutted sandy road.

One young man had no one with whom to go. He was orphaned. Samuel looked down at the young man, to the sad look on his face as the boy's people left their homes for good, some singing, some only groaning as they were bowed and trudging with old age. "Son, looks like you got nobody," Samuel said. He patted the boy on the shoulder and smiled. "Don't you worry. I'll take care of you." He pointed to his back yard. "You see that open space. We'll build you a house there."

"Thank you, sir." Jonas let out a relieved sigh. Now he would have somewhere to go.

He studied Samuel with a questioning look on his face. "What's your name" he finally asked.

"It's Brewton," Samuel answered.

"Well, then, that's my name too," Jonas said, then smiled.

The house was built. Jonas slept there, but every meal, he gathered around the table with Samuel and Mary Ann and their children. He became like one of the family.

As time went on, the family grew up and made homes of their

own. Samuel grew old. His hair and beard was now white. He'd always thought of Christianity as a roll-up-your-sleeves religion, and he and Mary Ann had raised Jonas.

When Samuel died, he left Jonas a one-horse farm and a large house. Eventually Jonas had a family then his family grew up. Finally he was left alone. "His family" that he'd grown up with, visited him. Then another generation came along and he became "Uncle Joe." They'd bring him turnip greens, other vegetables from their gardens, and quail in season.

In later years, Jonas would rock on his south facing front porch and visit his mule, "Old Gray," in the lot just a few yards to his right. They'd been together a long time.

Though Jonas was almost six feet and lean in stature, his body had now bowed somewhat and his hair was like white wool.

When he'd get enough of solitude, he'd hitch "Old Gray" to his black buggy and head to town. Both mule and man were too old to hurry. In fact, "Old Gray" was so old Jonas had lost count of his years. The mule could only stand stiff-legged, but the two were as close as any two friends could be.

In his late 90s, Jonas died. Prominent folks and friends, white and black, came from all around the area to Mt. Pleasant Church for his funeral.

Aubrey Strickland remembers going. He said the church was full. Anyone who wished to speak was asked to say a few words. Quite a few spoke of the old man, of his kindness, of his good disposition, and of his good advice.

It is said that when someone would come to him wanting money to get a husband or son out of jail, he'd ask, "What's the problem? Did they steal or did they hurt someone?" If the answer was "Yes," his answer was, "It's best they stay in jail, serve out their time." He didn't go in for wrongdoing.

As soon as the family came back from the long ride after the funeral, they went out to feed "Old Gray." This time "Old Gray" wasn't standing. He had passed away. One friend couldn't stay without the other. The family borrowed two mules from Charlie Strickland to pull the old mule off to bury him.

Because Jonas was a kindly man, thought well of, he is still remembered fondly. They still speak of Uncle Joe and his mule, Gray.

2

George Fagin Recalls the March of Sherman

Many years ago, an old man waited his turn at the cash register to pay for another pocketknife, his weekly ritual. He was short and dark, mid-sized with a deep bow to his back. His hands were knotty from hard work and arthritis. His dark face sagged with years, but he always had a light in his eyes as if he enjoyed every day.

"George, how are you?" I asked.

He smiled. "Fine, ma'am, just fine."

"George," I said. "You must be getting on up in age."

"Yes'um." He reached for his money and handed it to me for his knife. "I was a small boy when Sherman come through Claxton. Word had passed to us that he was coming. My whole body shook when I heard that."

For a moment he seemed to look back in time.

"My mama had us chillun grabbin our mattresses to carry them to the woods. We tied our mule in the middle of the deepest thicket, and the hogs had already been penned there."

He shook his head.

"We heard the thunder of all them horses' hooves before we saw them. My mama had us squatted in the bushes and she dared one of us to make a sound. We held onto one another and waited. When I saw them horses and the dust billowing behind, my heart felt like it would come out of my chest. My hands sweated and we held tight to one another. Mama said, 'You make one sound, and them men will come and take our food and maybe kill us too for hiding it.'"

Again he shook his head.

"I wanna tell you, Missus, as I squatted in them bushes, my feet burned so bad that tears ran down my face. In hurrying to get away, I'd stepped into a pile of ashes and both feet were scorched, the bottom skin burned through. That was long time ago, but I won't never forget it."

He stopped speaking as if he had just realized where he was. He tipped his hat. "Have a good day, Ma'am." He put his newly purchased pocket knife in his pants and left.

I stood there thinking how little we know of all life's trials that others go through.

3

Harley Was Put in the Well

Harley Brown heard a knock at the door. Ed Perry stood there.

"Harley, we're moving into the Baker Daniel house and need someone to clean out the well."

Harley hesitated. Cleaning out a well was dangerous. Sometimes there was poisonous gas in those old wells.

He scratched his head. It was hard times. He really needed the work. After all, he'd done all sorts of odd jobs for Miss Minnie, Mr. Perry's mother-in-law, and he'd helped Dr. Ben. Maybe he'd chance it.

The next morning he came up to the old long-unused farmhouse, and looking at it, wondered how they'd ever live there. There were saplings growing tall around every inch of the old house, a large fig tree and pear trees, but the grape arbor had fallen in and vines ran everywhere. He mused, at least they'd cut a path to the door, and Mr. Ed had poured more steps where the others had rotted.

He walked inside. There were cracks where the floor met the wall. He shook his head. There sure was lot of work to do or else they'd freeze. After all it was October already, and cold would soon set in. He also understood they had a young child they'd be trying to keep warm. The way the air poured through those cracks, they'd likely get pneumonia. Besides that, there was no electricity.

He walked on through the wide hall, onto the back porch. Steps to the back porch still had to be built.

Looking further, he saw the old well at the end of the covered porch. Would he be safe? How would he get down in there?

"I've drawn out most of the water, Harley, and we've put a foot-tub on the chain and braced the chain so you should be safe," Ed said. "We'll let you down in that."

Not so sure about what he was about to do, Harley looked long and hard at that well. The sides stood about four feet tall. How would he get up there to get in that bucket?

Ed, seeing his quizzical look said, "Harley, I'm strong. I'll get you up and hold the chain, even stand on the extra length as we let you down so you won't drop."

Harley eased over, looked at the depth and hoped he made it in and out.

Ed helped him in and Harley held tight as the bucket eased down. They dropped in another bucket for the trash. He touched bottom and started cleaning. He found frogs, bricks, limbs, and other trash in that icy cold water. So far he was doing fine, no poisonous gas.

Then he felt something. His fingers were cramped, wouldn't work. Was poison gas causing the problem? Scared, he hollered, "Get me out! I got the cramps. I may be gassed."

Quickly Ed pulled him up. Harley survived, but learned it was a case of cramps from the cold water, not poison gas.

At a later date, Harley went back to the old house and could hardly believe his eyes. Miss Mona had painted the kitchen chairs green, had black checked oilcloth on the table with wide baseboards covering the cracks and curtains over the windows. The old house was painted white; a wood stove crackled in the kitchen keeping it toasty warm; and that well was full of good clean water. They'd used Clorox to kill any germs.

Smiling, proud, Harley straightened. He'd helped a young couple get started in life on the farm and lived to tell about having been in the bottom of that deep well.

4

The Level School

There's a saying made famous by Robert Schuller that "Tough times don't last, but tough people do." Though tough times change from one challenge to another with time, Cora and her husband Thaddeus Hagan remembered fondly their days of attending school at "The Level," an unpainted school located close to what has come to be known as "The Level Church," about four miles south of Hagan, on Perry Road.

The Level settlement was started by Rev. Wyatt Kennedy about 1880 and was originally called Galilee, but was later named "The Level" by which it is still known.

According to Cora, they dressed early by lamp light, packed a syrup bucket with a couple of biscuits, a piece of fat-back, and maybe a piece of sweetbread or some syrup, and set out on the dirt road for school. Cora lived further south than Thaddeus out in what is known as the flatwoods, but both had to walk to school on narrow roads flanked on each side by tall pines and underbrush.

In dry times, dust rose with each step, and sand often filled their shoes. If hard rain came, they couldn't go to school. Teachers never knew if they would have as few as twenty or as many as fifty children present.

Cora and Thaddeus recalled different teachers over the years, some of whom had boarded with Thaddeus's parents, Mary and Cleve Hagan. They named Gladys Clark, Serena Kennedy, Ruby King, and Irene Spanns.

Pupils sat on homemade benches lined against each long wall behind homemade desks. In the center of the room was a potbellied stove. Cora said, "We nearly froze in the winter, but always managed to make it through 'til time to go home."

She smiled in remembrance. "We had enough books to learn from and some sort of rough paper to write on, and sometimes Blue Horse Composition books to write in.

School stopped after seventh grade. Not many made it that far, what with work and having to walk so far. Most pupils attended school a couple of days a week between field work – and only averaged attending about three months of the year."

She and Thaddeus recalled some students: Ruby Hagan, Purly and Jack Brown, Theodore and Tiny Boy Brown, Robert Williams, Willie Williams, Clifford Kennedy's children, and Reamer Kennedy's children.

Though the old school has long fallen into decay, Cora and Thaddeus felt going to school there enabled them to cope with the tough times of adulthood.

5

Anna Oxendine Washed for Miss Minnie and Ate Her Dumplings

Anna Oxendine worked for Miss Minnie Daniel. She'd worked for her for a long time, and both were now up in age.

Out in the back yard, she'd put the wash in a Number 2 washtub then put a fire beneath the wash pot and boiled the dirtiest clothes in lye soap water, "juging" them all along with a tobacco stick to keep them immersed.

Miss Minnie made her own lye soap and was proud of it. Anna watched her cut that cooled soap into bars for Anna to use on the clothes. Nothing got out stains like that lye soap.

While Anna washed and hung clothes on the line, her mouth salivated, thinking about those chicken and dumplings Miss Minnie was making for their dinner.

While Miss Minnie made dumplings, she also cooked the starch for Anna to starch the pillow cases, dresses, and tablecloths. Anna would immerse the special pieces in the cooked starch, and hang them on the line.

Meanwhile, Miss Minnie cooked the old rooster that she had killed and butchered and then waited until the meat was done before putting in the dumplings.

Once those clothes were on the line and drying, Miss Minnie called Anna inside. They sat around a large round oak dining table next to the kitchen and ate big helpings of mouth-watering chicken and dumplings, amply supplied with black pepper, the way they liked them. They also had cornbread and ice cold tea.

They'd gown old at the same time, but still worked well together, got the work done, and had good food.

What more could anyone want?

6

Axle Grease

It was about the year 1943. Ed Perry lived on a farm south of Hagan and it was always work time. He called to his help, "I noticed the wagon squealing a little, so we'll need to pull off the wheels one at a time and grease them."

He walked out to the shed where the wagon was kept along with tools and plows. "When we finish, we'll need to cut a load of wood for the fireplace and the wood stove."

The old man followed, never saying anything, but helped him remove the first wheel after they'd propped up that side of the wagon. "Look for a bottle of castor oil. I'm out of regular grease," Ed said.

The old man pretended to look, but then came back hanging his head. "Mr. Perry I'm sorry, but I put that oil on my pancakes."

Ed looked at him and shook his head and said, "Put it on pancakes! It's a wonder it didn't kill you." He said no more. What was there to say? "On his pancakes?"

They put the wheel back on and went after the wood. Greasing with axle grease could wait until another day.

7

Love, Kindness, and a Pot of Peas

In the Forties when the Ruthie Mae Davis family lived in the Perry pecan orchard about three hundred yards away from the Perry home. Ruthie Mae had several children and Mona Lee Perry had three at that time. It was hard times and hard work for everyone if families weren't to starve.

Ed planted a large garden and even with the children being so young, they had to help as best they could. They could pick peas and tomatoes, help with dishes, and even shell peas and butter beans. There was no such thing as food stamps back then. Everybody worked.

There came a day when Ruthie Mae had another baby. It was summer. Peas were on the vines. Mona sent her children to pick a large box of peas. They shelled enough to fill up a six-quart pressure cooker with ham hocks added. While those peas cooked, Mona made two hoecakes of cornbread. When that was done she sent her children to Ruthie Mae's with the peas and cornbread. With Ruthie Mae being unable to cook, at least they could fill up on peas and cornbread, and not be hungry.

Eventually, Mona had another baby, a girl, Patricia. There came a knock on the door. There stood Ruthie Mae with a pot of peas and a hoecake of cornbread.

Those were the days of love, kindness, and a pot of peas.

8

Son, Your Ma Ain't Learned to Save You Yet

Mona and Ed Perry lived on a farm out in Evans County. It was during World War II and there were many shortages. Even if they had the money to get goods, they weren't available. Anything from cars, tires, batteries, even gas was rationed. That meant there were also no phones out in the countryside. Mules and wagons were still being used on the farm. If you needed help to take care of an accident, you were on your own. Ed usually had the one car they owned off on the job.

Mona and Ed had three children, Chloe, Malcolm, and Ben, and also farm help who sometimes got hurt or overheated. Mona wondered what would happen.

Her children probably were the most vulnerable. Malcolm would take his tricycle and paddle wide open to sail off the high front porch into the shrubbery, not just once, but over and over. Ben was a follower, but even he managed somehow to set the curtains on fire even though there was a screen. Chloe fell against a rock and sprained her ankle. Something was always happening.

There were also other dangers. Mules were in one lot that could trample someone; cows could do the same in another; sows with new baby pigs were in the field; and trees had low-hanging limbs from which the children could fall.

With the children's having accidents and getting childhood diseases, Mona figured she'd better do something to improve the situation. About this time, a first-aid course was offered in town. That was her answer. She'd sign up. Then if someone got hurt, she might "doctor" them until she could get help. Still she couldn't leave her children. She had to have a sitter. Ed was busy with crops.

She asked around, and a young woman called "Doll Baby" said she'd sit the three. Satisfied, Mona left to take her course feeling her children would be safe while she was gone.

Doll Baby looked after them, but the two boys were as usual, curious about what was hidden, or wanted to know how something worked. Malcolm, wanting to see what was in the well on the back porch, managed to get up its four-foot side, and lean over.

Doll Baby spotted him and ran. She shouted "No!" and grabbed him by his heels when he was almost all the way over the side.

Down now, Malcolm stood there looking all innocent.

Still shaking Doll Baby stood in front of him, anger and fear on her face, and shook her finger. "Son," she said, "you can't do that. Your ma ain't learned to save you yet."

It was a toss-up as to who would need that first-aid course first, Doll Baby or Mona.

9

Our Easter Baskets Were Special

Allie Mae was the wife of Lawrence Bacon. In the 1940s she and Lawrence lived at the Perry Farm in a small, unpainted house that had a front room, kitchen, and shed room.

Allie Mae was always industrious. She used the cartoon section of the newspaper to cover one wall. She glued it with homemade paste made by cooking flour and water until it thickened into a paste. The cartoons brightened the unpainted room and helped insulate it.

She also undertook other projects. She decided to make a hat with corn shucks. Shucks were plentiful most of the year, and were either stored in the barn still around the ears of corn or came from the fields as fresh shucks. She needed a new hat for church. Taking those dried corn shucks, she cut the hard end off. Then she cut the shucks into pieces and braided them, sewed those braids into a crown, and added a flat brim. It needed more. She turned that hat around and around and decided that it would look good black. With a small can of black paint, she painted it. She still thought it required more. Then she added a few colorful dried flowers to one side and was ready for church.

The Perry children admired her hat. That's when she got the idea of making them something for Easter. She made three baskets with round bottoms, and then added a handle. Patricia was too small for one.

What a delight those baskets were for the children. They could hardly wait to show off their special Easter baskets and were especially proud that Allie Mae would go to all that trouble to make them. Every Easter those long-ago baskets that Allie Mae lovingly made, come to mind.

10

Cooter

Cooter was around five feet, with a slim, slightly bowed body and a kindly face. His eyes were furrowed, his cheekbones sagging with the weight of his years...years of field work and yard work.

The three children, two boys and a girl, watched as the tired old man trudged down the clay road to his weathered house across the road. His clothes were dusty and sandspurred with burrs from working the field. He murmured something and chuckles floated up from his throat. He threw back his head and let out a peal of noisy laughter.

The girl brought her hand up to stifle her giggles. She knew he was laughing at the joke he had pulled on the three children. Being tired had never stopped him from teasing. This time it would be their turn.

They watched the even tread of his feet until he approached his house and walked up the small incline into the brush-broom-clean dirt yard surrounding his small house next to the branch. He stopped at his steps, pulled out his can of Prince Albert tobacco and his rolling papers, and made a cigarette. After he wet the paper with his tongue to seal it, he stuck it into his mouth and struck a match to light it. His hands cupped the flame. A ravel of smoke curled and lost itself in the air. Standing there, he took another draw, and then let out the smoke through his nose. He seemed in no hurry. The workday was over and there was no one to come home to.

He walked up the two steps and across the wood porch to a water shelf on the side next to the woods. Holding the cigarette between his lips, he primed the pump and patiently pumped a pan of water. There was a quiet that wasn't really silent, a buzz of flies, the distant chatter of a squirrel in the woods, and the trilling calls of birds. He splashed water on his face and arms and dried them on the worn towel hanging on a nail.

In moments he unlocked his heavy wood door and listened as it squealed a protest while he pushed it back against the wall. The day hadn't yet let go of its heat.

The children listened as sounds came from the inside. The wooden window shutter creaked and moved back against the outside wall. The old man's hand reached out the window to the wood shelf for a splinter or two and a short length of wood. In moments, a puff of smoke rose from the chimney. It was a good way to run mosquitoes out. Soon there was a flash of light as the low flame of a kerosene lamp flared.

Shadows lengthened. What light there was seemed to be a pinkish gray. The first stars began to twinkle. There was a rustling of undergrowth and the rattling of tree limbs. An owl hooted, its eerie cry coming from not far away.

The older boy licked his lips and rubbed his fingers together time after time and waited. Finally the time was right. By silent agreement, the three were ready for their prank. The older boy pulled the rosin-coated string of the whang-doodle. A spine-tingling sound emitted from the tin can.

All movement ceased in the little house. The boy pulled the string again, and listened as the moaning wail rose even louder this time.

Moments later, a kerosene lamp light flickered by the window. The old man called out, "Who's that?" In the shadow of the light, trying to discern any movement, he turned his head towards the sound. Not hearing any more, he moved cautiously to the front door which still stood open. He walked out and looked around.

Something rustled in the brush near the edge of the trees, "Children, is that you?"

Smiles turned up the corners of the children's mouths. They made no sound, but pulled the string again sliding their fingers once more to make the ominous sound.

The front door slammed. The bolt snapped into place. Next the window creaked as Cooter closed and locked it. The children held their laughter until they eased out of Cooter's hearing, then laughed so hard their sides hurt.

About this time, their mother called them to come in from play. They turned to see the soft flow of their one overhead bulb shining from their living room window. It was time to go, but they figured their friend would guess that they'd paid him back for all the teasing he'd done to them.

Baker Daniel House. (Acrylics on canvas). This house, located about one-half mile south of Hagan, later became the Perry family home. It had four bedrooms, parlor, large hall, dining room, kitchen, and covered back porch.

Time Passes By. (Acrylics on canvas).

Tobacco Barn. (Acrylics on canvas).

Ducks on the Pond. (Acrylics on canvas).

Wagon and Hay Barns. (Acrylics on canvas).

Once a Country Store. (Acrylics on canvas).

The Lonely Tree. (Acrylics on canvas).

Abandoned. (Acrylics on canvas).

Left. The Outside Reading Room. (Acrylics on canvas). Every farm had at least one of these.

The Perry Pond adjacent to the Mitchell home on Perry Road about one-half mile south of Hagan provides a "ghostly" appearance in early mornings and late evenings. See Chapter 11. (Photo by Pharris Johnson)

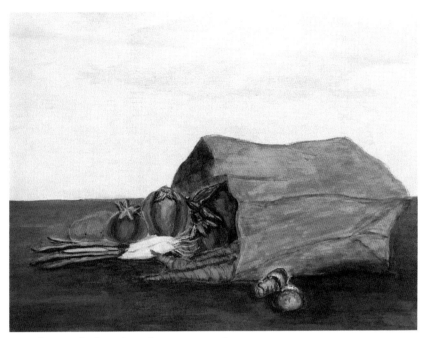

Garden Delights. (Acrylics on canvas).

Another photo of the Perry Pond shows it can be quite alluring on a summer day as described in Chapter 16. Its serene beauty makes it a landmark in the Hagan community. (Photo by Pharris Johnson)

The Level Church, about 4 miles south of Hagan on Perry Road, also known as Eureka Congregationalist Church later became Mount Zion Methodist. The structure now is near collapse. (2013 photo courtesy Brian Brown, Vanishing South Georgia).

Interior of The Level Church. It featured the pale green wainscoted walls typical of many vernacular churches dating from the late 1800s. (2013 photo courtesy Brian Brown, Vanishing South Georgia).

According to local tradition, Reverend Wyatt Kennedy founded the Eureka Congregationalist Church at The Level about 1880. The community grew in the surrounding area. (2013 photo courtesy Brian Brown, Vanishing South Georgia).

Located across the road from the remains of The Level's Eureka Church is the church's cemetery. Pictured is the tombstone of Rev. B. H. Hughes, Sr., (1896-1955). Many of the African-American people described in this book's pages are buried in the cemetery. (2013 photo courtesy Brian Brown, Vanishing South Georgia.)

The Level's school was known as Eureka. The historic school included industrial arts and some students worked at a nearby cannery. (Photo from Dottie Simmons Collection.)

A typical house in The Level. (Ink on paper).

Preaching and Teaching. (Acrylics on canvas). Life in The Level community revolved around the area's church and school.

From left: Reamer Kennedy, Penny Kennedy and Lewis "Luke" Kennedy. Luke and his wife were freed slaves who purchased land in what became The Level community. They raised 14 children and were charter members of Mount Zion Methodist Church. (Photo from Dottie Simmons Collection.)

JONAS BREWTON

Jonas Brewton, colored, died at his home in Evans county, Saturday, May 20th, at the age of 95 years.

Jonas was a slave of the late Sam Brewton, who was the grand father and relative of many of the prominent families of Claxton and this section, a fact which made Jonas known to so many of the white citizens.

These white friends say that Jonas' life was a good example to his race, that he lead a clean life. At his funeral the statement was made that he served as deacon of one church for 60 years. Many fine testimonies were given by people who knew him and by white frienns.

The deceased was very active for his mature years and lived alone in his comfortable home, doing all the chores himself.

Jonas Brewton was probably a child of a slave of Nathan Brewton and was inherited by Nathan's youngest son Samuel. By Christmas of 1864, many of the slaves left. Jonas had no place to go, so he stayed, took the name Brewton, and virtually became a family member. On Samuel's death, he left Jonas a farm. As told in the first chapter in this book, a strange and fascinating fact is that Jonas' mule, "Gray" died the same day as Jonas. Jonas' obituary appeared on the front page of *The Claxton Enterprise* on May 25, 1939.

Samuel Brewton (1819-1887). Much of the land where this book's stories are set, at one time belonged to Samuel. As Tattnall County deed books indicate (this area was in Tattnall before Evans County was created), he acquired thousands of acres of land through grants, inheritance, and purchase. Samuel was an industrious plantation owner who also served in the state of Georgia Legislature from 1859-1860.

Mittie Brown "Doll Baby" worked for Mona Lee Perry as a baby sitter. Mattie was wise beyond her years.

Numerous African-American residents worked in tobacco farming. Here ladies and children unload the field sleds and string green leaves in preparation for curing in the barn. This rare photo is from the Lucile Hodges Collection at Georgia Southern Library.

Many African-American women excelled at sewing and quilting. and some were very higly skilled. Scraps, discarded clothing, and feed sacks, were often the materials used. The maker of this quilt is Virginia Brewton, grandmother of Evans County resident Patrica Milton. (Quilt photo courtesy of Patricia Milton.)

11

The Pond Was Ghostly

It was about the year 1950. Herman and Lillie Belle lived in a small house north of the former Baker Daniel Pond. The house was about 450 yards from where Herman had to pick up the tractor at the shelter at the Perry's and walk past that pond.

The Perry children noticed that Herman and Lilly Belle acted strange when they had to walk by that pond and over the small bridge to get to the tractor shelter. In fact, neither would walk past that pond unless he had a staff at least six feet long and two inches in circumference, nor would they walk past that pond after dark. The children figured they had to be scared, but of what?

When asked why, Lilly Belle said, "Ghosts come out of that pond and those big sticks protect us."

The children had long noticed there was often a low-hanging fog over the pond in early morning and again at twilight. This mist and haze made it sort of scary, in fact ghostly, but they'd never seen any ghosts.

Still every time Lilly Belle and Herman walked by that pond even in bright daylight, they'd watch warily and hurry on as fast as they could walk, then let out a great breath once they passed it.

Many a time Chloe, Malcolm, Ben and Patricia watched as the two almost ran to get past that pond. Finally they asked their mother if there was any such thing as ghosts. Mona said she'd been told that a member of the Coley family accidentally ran into that pond in an early model car and drowned. She understood it was an uncle of Thornton Coley.

The children puzzled over that. Lilly Belle and Herman had never heard that story. Maybe they had seen a ghost. Who would know?

12

Ernest Has a New Job

In the 1940s, Ernest Mitchell and his Geechee wife lived in a little house across the Perry Pond north of the Perry home. Ernest did whatever chores on the farm he was assigned.

Mona and Ed had four children, the first three close in age and all had the usual childhood illnesses such as chicken pox, measles, mumps, colds, and whatever else there might be.

One of the children broke out with the measles and Mona hoped by not exposing the others any more than necessary, they might not catch them. She needed help to keep the children outside, but with one sick she couldn't watch them all. Being on a busy farm, her energetic children could get hurt if they weren't watched. What must she do? Then it came to her. Ed agreed it would work.

She asked Ernest to let the three well children ride around in the farm wagon while she looked after Chloe. Mona dosed Chloe with sassafras tea to break out the measles so they wouldn't settle in her system and made sure to keep the room dark. Ernest drove Malcolm, Ben, and Patricia all over the farm. He went from one job to another, putting out corn for the chickens, feeding the mules and hogs, and kept the children occupied while the wagon ambled along lulling them and satisfying them for the day.

Came the day when Chloe was well, but then Malcolm and Patricia broke out with the red bumps. Mona sighed. "Ernest, I suppose you'll have to ride the well ones while I take care of these other two."

"Yes, Ma'am," he said, and smiling helped them up onto the wagon and away they went. He looked after one and another until the measles had gone the rounds.

They never misbehaved. Ernest smiled. He guessed he'd helped and that certainly had been a new job for him....baby sitting.

13

Mary Hagan Was Never Known to Waste

Mary Hagan was the mother of Thaddeus Hagan and lived next door to Thaddeus and Cora out on Perry Road. She was a tiny woman that kept busy doing whatever she needed to do, even when she was up in years. She believed in using what you had and not being in debt.

She'd take old clothes that were too small, had holes in them, small scraps, any materials that she could use to make quilts to keep the family warm. She'd cut them into odd pieces, sew them together, and make a quilt top.

If she had cotton, she'd use that for batting. If she had an old quilt too worn and scraggly to use, she'd use that as the batting and add backing to finish the quilt.

In winter, she'd sit by the fire to quilt, but as soon as it was warm enough, she'd move her quilt frame outside beneath an old oak tree. There she would pull up a chair, sit there, and quilt by the natural light. Her family and friends would see her there running her needle in and out stitching around those pieces she'd put into the quilt. She sewed beautiful patterns, or whatever the quilt needed. Sometimes she even made these treasures for others when asked.

Whether she needed the quilts or not, she knew her children or grandchildren would need them for warmth and nothing was going to waste as long as she was able to do something with the scraps. Her motto was "Waste not, want not."

Mary is long gone now, but I still remember her sitting under that oak tree quilting when she was too old to do much else.

14

Bob Small Gets Lost

Bob Small, father of Cora Hagan lived just off the old Hagan-Glennville Road, an unpaved thoroughfare past Bay Branch Road. He was 104 years old, but active. This particular day, his goal was to go to the flatwoods, a large section of woods south of Bay Branch Road to cut firewood.

Farmers sometimes rented this large section of woods for their cattle to graze. Ed Perry had seen a small bear in there that slept beneath a sheet of tin which leaned against an old dilapidated tobacco barn. There were also bobcats and other wild animals. Though they could be dangerous, Bob wasn't scared. He had his axe with him.

Bob hitched his wagon and headed out. Later in the day, the man came for his load of wood, but there was none and no sign of Bob. That worried him. Bob had never gone back on his promise and at his age, anything could have happened to the old man. The man decided to wait a while, but as time rolled on, there was still no sign of Bob. It was time to call in help.

Loren Waters was sheriff at the time and got out the word he needed help to look for a lost man. Time was of the essence in case the old man was ill, hurt, or just lost.

Lots of people answered the call and looked for hours. By late afternoon, they had found no trace of him, but as they were about to give up for the day, they received a call. Bob had come out on the Mendes Road and someone by the name of Sands called in that Bob was safe.

When questioned, Bob said, "I figured if I kept going in those woods I'd have to come out to a road somewhere."

Thing is, most of us would have kept going in circles. However, he'd proven his wisdom by not giving up. Moreover, Bob learned how much people in the community cared for his welfare.

15

Herman Tries to Outwit the Bulldog

It was a beautiful day in late spring. Herman (Smith?) sang along as he drove the large Farmall Tractor from the Clanton field by his house, crossed the Perry Pond, and drove south on up the hill past the house of his boss, Ed Perry. A few feet further, he moved past the old Baker Daniel white clapboard house to the field gate where he was to plant peas between the pecan trees in the orchard. He'd be planting the whole field. That way the Perrys and all their farm workers could pick all they wanted when the peas matured.

He stopped at the wooded gate to enter the field. In his mind he saw those peas coming to maturity and himself coming home to a large pot of them with ham hocks that Lilly Belle had cooked, along with a large glass of tea. What more could a man want?

Right now he hadn't a care in the world. He'd plant those peas. Then his day would be over, and he'd head home.

Just as he started to step down from the tractor to open the gate, he spotted his nemesis, Zip. Zip was the Perry daughter, Chloe's, bulldog. The dog sat upright in a large white rocker on the Perry porch watching her surroundings right behind Miss Mona's long containers of red geraniums. The red of those geraniums made him think of how red the blood would be on his skin if he couldn't find a way to open that wooden gate and get into that field. It was only a hundred yards from that house to the tractor. Zip could get there before he could pull that gate open and get back up on the tractor. Shinnying up a tree or jumping a fence wasn't something he wanted to do. So, how could he get through that gate? If he didn't hurry he wouldn't finish and could lose his job. He sat there, the tractor chugga-lugging while he tried to figure what to do.

Glancing back at the width of the tractor sticking out behind him an idea hit, but before he could move, Zip was there. Her fangs were showing, and her stance intimidating. Thing was, he'd never figured why Zip didn't like him. She never bothered Cooter Mincey, Theron, Willie, or Troy Anderson. Why him? He couldn't ponder all day though. He had to make his move and hoped his plan worked.

He shook his head and laughed, "Old girl, you won't have a chance at me this time. I have a plan."

Zip didn't back off.

Time was wasting. Herman put the tractor in reverse and backed up a few feet. Then with enough room, he turned the tractor around, reversed again, then backed up to that wooded gate. With his right hand, he held the steering wheel. With his left, he grabbed that gate and held on, praying he had the strength to move that heavy gate enough to open it with only one hand.

Little by little, it eased open.

Zip sat back on her haunches and watched.

Herman sped forward, turned around and eased through. He wanted to smile, but dared not. He hadn't totally succeeded yet.

Backing up at an angle, again he grabbed that gate. He pulled it, eased forward, finally got it closed.

He glanced back. Zip still hadn't figured that one out. Laughing heartily, Herman gunned the gas. His laughter echoed in that large pecan orchard while he hooked up the planter and headed down the rows planting peas. What a day! He'd outsmarted Zip.

16

Their Swim Had Unintended Results

In the summer of 1951, Malcolm Perry and Herman Smith were moseying along toward the Perry home carrying a bucket they'd used in the Clanton Field north of Herman's house. It was hot, late afternoon. They were dirty, tired, and sweaty. About to pass the family pond, they spotted that cool pond water. One dared the other to pitch that bucket into the deep side and dive for it. They were having a good time diving for the bucket and cooling off with no worries.

Shorty Neal from Hagan passed, saw them go down and gunned his engine to hurry to the Perry home. Fearing they'd drowned, he leaned on the doorbell.

Mona answered the door.

"Mrs. Perry," he said breathlessly, "I passed the pond. Your son and another man were going down for the third time."

Mona, fearing for her son's life, grabbed her keys, jumped into her car and roared down the dirt road to the pond. A cloud of dust billowed behind her. She fully expected to see her son's body floating on the water or having to get divers to find him in that dark water. She slammed on brakes, jumped out of her car and to her surprise Malcolm and Herman came up laughing and swimming vigorously.

Needless to say, those two were out shortly, with dry clothes on, and were put back to work. That was their last swim at the Perry Pond.

17

Where's the Cabbage?

In the 1950s many people grew vegetable gardens and when they produced, the family ate what was grown, canned some, froze some, dried some, and shared.

Between 1950-1954, the Perry's garden was about one-and-a-half acres with squash, onions, Irish potatoes, cucumbers, cantaloupes, tomatoes, cabbage, butter beans, peas, beets, mustard greens, and turnip greens, in season.

Somehow, Cooter Mincey, (Virgil), a thin man who lived on the Perry Farm, always managed to let his paycheck get away from him on weekends, leaving him with no money for food. Ed Perry, knowing his wife always cooked plenty told Mona, "If Cooter is to work, he has to be fed." So everyday Cooter came inside the glassed-in back porch at the Perry's for dinner.

This particular time, the garden was prolific with cabbage that had huge, tight heads. That's when Mona made vegetable soup with it, or slaw, and on other days, cooked cabbage. Nothing was wasted. When Cooter came in, he found his plate piled high with cabbage plus, all the other vegetables, meat, bread, and plenty of iced tea.

While starting dinner one day, Mona decided enough was enough. Even though there were many more heads of cabbage to be cut, she figured everyone was tired of eating cabbage.

Cooter came in at noon, sat down at the table where he always ate his meals, and ate the plate full that was set before him. He finished, took the last swallow of tea, and then said, "Miss Mona Lee, it was all good, but where's the cabbage?"

18

There's Music and Then There's Music

We all have our loves and likes. Herman and Lilly Belle lived on the Perry Farm north of the family pond in a small, unpainted tenant house. It had a front room with a fireplace, a kitchen, and a shed room with just the necessary furnishings and on the front porch a wash shelf with a hand pump. They had little, but were happy. Much of this happiness was found in the finest juke box around. It had all of Herman's favorite records.

That juke box was tall, huge, and had a red glass surround. When you punched the record you wanted, the arm would swing across with that record. With Herman's doors and windows open, it could be heard many yards away. Listening was Herman's pride and joy.

Malcolm, one of the Perry children, loved music and loved playing the few 78 rpm records he had. His mother, wanting her children to play the piano, mostly bought sheet music of gospel, popular, or church hymns, so the children could play and the family sing around the piano.

Wanting a new record or two, but with no spending money, Malcolm went to Herman's house after work. He'd bargain three of his records for three of Herman's. All he had to trade was "The Tennessee Waltz," "The Kentucky Waltz," and a polka.

Herman agreed to the trade.

With it being steamy outside and in 1951, the windows were open. Smiling, Malcolm heard a cow moo for her calf, a pig squeal and a hen cackle that she'd laid an egg. However, his mind was on getting upstairs to listen to his new records, not on what was going on outside.

He hurried upstairs to the Victrola, put the first record on, grabbed the handle to wind the spring, then put the needle down to play. He stood there enjoying his record.

Mona, his mother, was picking figs when she heard this loud music, "Hey, Jim Dandy. Hey, Jim Dandy. What make your big head so hard?" Her mouth gaped wide open. Where was that music coming from?

It wasn't long before Malcolm was carrying those 78s back and by that time, Herman had decided the records Malcolm traded weren't his favorite kind of music either.

As Malcolm walked out of Herman's house, Herman already had his beloved music on. "Hey, Jim Dandy..."

Author's note: We think Herman's last name was Smith.

19

There's More Than One Way to Skin a Catfish

It was mid-July 1957 and hot, tobacco picking and curing days. Virgil Mincey, known as Cooter, wiped the sweat which had puddled on his forehead. At the same time he wondered if his boss, Mr. Perry, would survive the major heart attack he'd had while checking the heat in one of the tobacco barns. These barns cured the tobacco at high temperature. His boss was only forty-four, but Cooter had already heard it said that rest for two months was the only treatment of the time. Cooter scratched his head. He wanted to do something, but what could he do to help? He had no money.

He knocked on the Perry's door.

The door opened.

"Miss Mona Lee, could I see Mr. Perry?" He noticed she looked harried as if she was worn out from all the extra work.

"Sorry, Cooter," she said. "Dr. Hames said no visitors, not even family any more than necessary." She shook her head, "Dr. Hames doesn't want him to talk."

"I'm sorry, Ma'am."

She closed the door.

Cooter went on back to work. Was there anything he could do? Was there anything that would cause no harm, but something that would cost nothing? They'd been mighty good to him.

He continued to work, but then a smile crossed his face. He had an idea.

He went home, prepared, then came back and knocked on the Perry's door.

Mona answered.

"Miss Mona Lee, could you open Mr. Perry's window?" She looked puzzled.

I wanted to do something for Mr. Perry and thought I would sit on a stool outside his window and play and sing him a few songs." He hesitated. "That wouldn't hurt none, would it?"

Mona smiled. "Get your stool, Cooter and I'll open the window. A little music won't hurt."

Cooter set up a stool he got from under the garage and then sat down to play his guitar. "Oh, my bucket's got a hole in it. Oh, my bucket's got a hole in it. Oh, my bucket's got a hole in it. I can't buy me no beer."

Mona watched as Ed smiled.

Cooter sang another song about pork chops and then eased away, wondering if he'd hurt or helped his boss.

The next time he saw Miss Mona she said, "Thank you, Cooter. He enjoyed your songs."

The corners of Cooter's mouth turned up. One of the old sayings his pa had was "There's always more than one way to skin a catfish." Cooter surmised that if you couldn't find one way to do something, there was always another way.

His boss lived six more years.

20

What Am That I Smell

"Cooter" Virgil Mincey, was of medium height, slim, and his hair cropped short. He was probably getting close to his sixties, but strong from working on the Ed Perry Farm. In the 1950s, he lived in a small house, just large enough for his needs across the road and down the hill from his boss. He was always ready to do whatever he needed to do on the farm. His jobs ranged from picking cotton, hoeing weeds, feeding the cows, or whatever came up to do. Jobs were portioned out to all the farm workers.

On this particular day, his job was to ride on the one-and-a-half-ton truck with Theron Anderson to Savannah to pick up a load of fertilizer. This time of year the weather was hot, gnats were buzzing and there was no such thing as air-conditioning in those work trucks. If you wanted air, you rode with the windows open.

Farm work was hard, and the days long. When a chance for a few minutes rest came along, one rested even if it was only minutes. After loading the fertilizer in Savannah, and now on the way back, Cooter saw his chance to rest. He lay on top of the load of fertilizer. He could get the breeze and stretch out for a nap for the hour's ride home.

Theron took their usual road home. Cooter was already sound asleep when his nose twitched. He smelled a strong odor. It was so overwhelming, he raised up, glanced around, and sniffed again. "Whew!" he said, then he turned towards the cab of the truck, and hollered "Cleon," over the roar of the truck, "What am that I smell?"

Theron smiled and said, "Cooter that's the tannery hide house."

Theron, laughing at Cooter's adventure, told the Perry family about Cooter's reaction. We still laugh about it today.

21

Rosa's Aggravating Goat

Rosa and Willie Brewton lived on a one-horse farm left to Willie by his father, Jonas Brewton. It was just past the farm of Jerome Glisson, near a location that became the county dump. Their old, unpainted house was a shotgun structure with a wide hall and a kitchen attached by a long porch. The porch's west side was walled and the east side open with steps to the ground.

Rosa was short, slightly rotund but with a wonderful sense of humor. She always came to work neatly dressed with her hair tied with a red bandanna with a knot in the front at her hairline. In fact, Rosa looked something like Hattie in *Gone With the Wind* except she was of lighter complexion. She sometimes liked to tell, as she ironed, about happenings at her house. Then she'd chuckle and shake a little as she told her stories.

One day she came to work, and as she was ironing said, "Mrs. Mitchell, I got to tell you what happened yesterday." She spit a mouthful of snuff into her now empty Navy snuff can. "I was home all day working in the kitchen cooking and washing dishes when I went out on the porch to get Irish potatoes out of a croaker sack for dinner. That's when I noticed some had gone to the bad, but there were enough to cook. I just left the sack with those bad potatoes there for the time being.

Later I heard our old goat baaing. I looked out and there he was in the yard. He had gotten over the fence somehow and was out of the field, again. That aggravating goat was always getting out, and into stuff. Willie asked to keep him. So I decided if that's what he wanted, let him get the old goat back in the field. I went on with my cooking.

After a while, I heard that goat baaing again and looked out, but he didn't seem to be into anything. Maybe he was hungry or had gotten into something he shouldn't have.

Later I heard him baaing loudly like he was hurting, but I checked and still saw nothing unusual. Sometimes he baaed like that for no reason that I could see.

I had just gotten back into the kitchen and had my hands in the dishwater when I heard Pow! What was that? Hearing the explosion, I ran outside."

Rosa looked disbelieving then said, "That old goat was lying there – busted wide open." She scratched her head and continued, "He'd got into that sack of soured potatoes and eaten his fill."

"You mean he actually exploded," I asked.

"Sure did. Those sour potatoes swole him up and blew him to pieces."

"Was he still alive?" I asked.

She sprinkled water onto the piece of clothes she was ironing then looked up and said, "Dead as a mackerel, and smelled like rotten potatoes." She shook her head, raised her brows, and then turned the piece of clothes to iron another part. "I guess he won't be getting out of that fence and aggravating me no more."

22

Jack Littles Hacked with His Axe

Jack Littles worked hard. He had to make a living. Whatever he was able to do he did with little education.

John Mitchell hired him to cut up stumps for lightered wood, or kindling, as some know it. Quite a few stumps were in the Mitchell woods, and the lightered would come in good for fires in the fireplace. Jack set his price and figured he'd have money to buy groceries.

He took the axe, worked his way into those thick woods and cut for several days. When he finished one late afternoon, he came out for his money.

He and John met. John handed him the agreed upon amount including some bigger bills.

Jack wiped his forehead with his bandanna and said, "Uh-uh, can't have that."

It took a minute for John to catch on as to what he was getting at. He reached into his pocket and came out with the same amount in ones and handed them to Jack.

Jack looked at them, counted the bills and smiled contently.

23

Sometimes Life Holds a Few Shocks

With his sleeves rolled up and sweat popping out on his forehead from heat and exertion, R. S. Lovett cut and piled timber. The day was muggy, hot, and the sky, gray. These were indications of an approaching thunderstorm, but R.S. figured as long as it wasn't pouring or lightning nearby, he could take care of a few more trees. His logging operation couldn't afford too much down time.

The afternoon wore on. In the distance, thunder rumbled, and wind now whistled in the pines. Increasingly, the thunder sounded closer. From his seat on the tractor, he noticed a few flickers of lightning in the far distance. He shrugged. It was still a ways off. He had a while longer. He could continue.

A bolt of lightning suddenly zigzagged its signature across the sky and snapped. Thunder rolled.

R.S. sucked in a breath. That bad weather was closing in.

The sky darkened.

That got his attention. Glancing up, he said to himself, "Just one more tree. I can do that much."

He put his tractor in gear, rolled up with precision to the next tree and clamped large metal jaws around the trunk. So far, so good, he thought.

Another jagged splinter of lightning lit the sky, ran down that tree, thunder rolling with it. That bolt ran through those long, metal arms and jaws, jolted him, and ran up into the tractor, shaking R.S. 'til his teeth rattled.

He hung on.

As fast as electricity running through a power line, tires exploded and rent the air with pieces of rubber flying everywhere. The tractor sank to the ground.

"Run!" R. S. hollered. Sprinting, he touched ground and hopped logs and brush. Lightning popped behind him every step as he headed to his truck.

His body quaking, almost too shaky to jerk the door open, he yanked and jumped in. He sat there aghast, trying to draw a shaky breath before moving out. Taking one last look, he saw his tractor sitting on the ground with nothing but metal wheels, pieces of tires smoldering, and rain coming in torrents. He cranked his truck to leave, still shaky, and hardly able to believe how lucky he had been.

As he drove home, he told himself, "This day will live in my memory a long time."

24

Annie Gets Put in the Deep Freeze

Willie and Annie Strowbridge did yard work for Mona Perry Allen. They worked in the daylilies, cut grass, weeded, sprayed daylilies and camellias, picked up sticks, trimmed shrubbery, picked up pecans in season, and whatever else came up to be done in the yard and did other chores when asked.

After Willie died, Frank, their son, worked along with Annie. Willie had been slim, fragile, and old, but willing to work, and now that he was gone, their son, strong and tall, worked beside Annie, doing the same chores that Willie had done.

Annie was small, probably 85-90 pounds, wizened, but didn't mind working for Miss Mona Lee almost daily. However, sometimes she was called on to do a chore the men weren't asked to do. This particular day, Miss Mona had another job especially for Annie.

Mona was widowed, so Chloe would call every day to check on her. Knowing her mother was always busy doing something, she asked, "What are you up to this morning?

Mona said, "Oh, I just put Annie in the freezer."

"You what?" Chloe wondered what Annie could possibly have done to get put in the deep freeze? She and Mona had never had words, though Annie could sometimes get vocal when she thought she wasn't going to get the particular croaker sack she wanted to put her pecans in. Did she actually freeze Annie?

At that point, Mona caught on to what she'd said, and laughed. "That freezer is so deep we couldn't reach bottom, so I put Annie in to get the food out."

"Oh," Chloe said, hardly able to wait to tell her brothers and sister about their mother putting Annie in the freezer.

Now when Mona's children clean out their freezer, they're reminded of the time their mother put Annie in the deep freeze and what Chloe first thought her mother might have done. They then have a hearty laugh.

25

Rosa's Advice

The Perry children grew up and left home. Chloe married, lived in town, and by now she had her second child. Rosa Brewton not only had helped when the Perry children were growing up, but now helped with Chloe's children.

This particular day, the new baby, Keith was only days old. Having been brought up to keep on going no matter what, Chloe was busy working in the house and taking care of the baby.

Rosa cooked, and then started ironing.

About this time, Chloe started crying. She could go no longer.

Rosa propped her iron and looked at Chloe. "Mrs. Mitchell, God gives us a certain amount to do in this life, but He gives us time to do it."

Chloe listened.

Rosa then brushed a damp cloth across the piece she was ironing. "We can hurry and get it done and go on...or we can take our time and be here a while longer to get it all done."

Chloe would never forget Rosa's words of advice.

Index

Note: Numbers in italics indicate illustrations.

Long Days of Summer in Evans County

You rise before the dawn

You're tired and ail,

But, as you dress, you see the day come alive softly,

While it pauses lightly on your windowsill.

Clothes on now, you watch the moving shadows

Lighten…

The sky changes slowly turning to blue-grey,

You have work to do but listen through the distant

Darkness

To songbirds greet the day.

As they are, be happy you're here.

Watch the day's light grow and widen,

Though early day hides the workday sun…The day is long,

While you hoe, pick tobacco, break corn, and

Other chores, but

In your heart you can still feel blessed,

God's gift to you… today…has come,

In Evans County

Chloe Perry Mitchell

91231834R00046

Made in the USA
Columbia, SC
14 March 2018